New Zealand GolfCross

NEW ZEALAND
GOLFCROSS

ORIGINATION O PRESS

WELLINGTON

ORIGINATION PRESS
487 Karaka Bay Road
Wellington, 6003
New Zealand

The moral right of Burton Silver to be identified as the creator of this work including the ball, tee cup and the game of golfcross has been asserted by him in accordance with the Copyright, Designs, and Patents Act, 1988.

GolfCross® is a registered trademark of Conclusion Ltd and the unique and distinctive dimpled oval golf ball shape is also a trademark of Conclusion Ltd. GolfCross is a patented game.

Photographs & text, Burton Silver. Illustrations & Design, Burton Silver & Heather Busch.
Editorial, Martin O'Connor.
Photograph page 12, Annelies Vanderpoel.

ISBN: 0 – 9597716 – 6 – 2

First NZ printing, 2001, printed and bound in China.

3   4   5—05   04

GolfCross Website: www.golfcross.com

CONTENTS

Preface   7

Introduction   8

The Making of the Game   13

The Oval Ball   19

The Game of GolfCross   33

Designing a Course   47

Two Courses: 68

    Station Bush   71

    Braemar Station   79

Etiquette   86

Rules   88

Glossary   93

Acknowledgements   96

PREFACE

A white, dimpled, grass-stained ball is nestled on the turf – a club poised behind it. This is such a familiar golfing scene that it takes a moment to realize there's something odd about it. Suddenly it registers. The ball is oval like a football and, as you rapidly scan the rest of the image for an explanation, you see the goal posts in the distance. Then you smile.

When something we have been very familiar with all our lives is radically changed it's always unsettling. It challenges our secure view of the world and we instinctively dismiss what we're seeing as some kind of joke. We laugh, we shake our heads and then, in this crazy world, we move on.

This book has been written in the hope that you'll stay a little longer. Stay and discover the secrets of the oval golf ball and the game of New Zealand GolfCross. Maybe you'll even be inspired to set up a course.

Remember, nobody believes that the oval ball is more controllable than a round one – until they hit it. Even we were not prepared for the distinctive high pitched hum that accompanies the spinning ball on its journey down the fairway. It seemed that a ball so smart it would do what we asked and sing its own praises was just too good to be true. And every golfer is amazed to discover that all the control properties they've ever wanted have been hiding in the oval ball all the time. Even the golf ball makers are surprised.

Just think, if you can play an exciting round of golf with a ball that most would have considered completely unsuitable for the task, imagine what other new golfing challenges might be discovered in the future.

Burton Silver, Wellington, 2001.

INTRODUCTION

Golfcross is golf in everything but shape. It's played over a course just like golf, using the same clubs and the same rules. Only two things are different – the shape of the ball and the shape of the target.

Hold the golfcross ball in your hand and you're unmistakably holding a golf ball. It has the same smooth white dimpled exterior you know so well and it's about the same size and weight. What makes it so intriguing is that it's oval instead of round.

For more than 500 years golf balls have been as perfectly spherical as we can make them.

So why, you may ask, would anybody want to mess with something that has such a proven record? Have we somehow had it wrong for five centuries? Not at all. The round ball is exactly right for golf which, like soccer, requires that it be played along the ground as well as in the air. Nothing but a perfectly round ball can be accurately putted across the smooth surface of a green and into a hole. But if a game has no need for the ball to roll towards a target, then the oval shape, which is easier to control and capable of more flight path variations, becomes

an interesting alternative.

Like rugby or American football, golfcross is an aerial game with a target that's raised above the turf. Golf's round hole, set in the ground to receive the rolling ball, is replaced by a new shape – the rectangular goal suspended in mid-air to trap the flying ball. With no putting, the game is not confined to using a round ball. It allows us to play golf with an oval ball and, for the first time, enjoy its advanced performance capabilities.

Because it's aerodynamically more stable than a golf ball there are things you can do

with a golfcross ball that can make a game of golf a whole lot more interesting. For example, being able to hit the ball straight every time means being able to confidently play a driver from the fairway and decide whether you want your ball to stop or run on simply by setting it upright or leaning it back. Controlled slices and hooks are easily achieved – as are various degrees of fade and draw – by angling the ball to the side.

This means that golfers can now spend time planning their attack, knowing that they're in control with a ball that will behave the way they want it to, rather than the way *it* wants to.

However, what the golfcross ball gives with one hand, its course design takes away with the other. The ball may be smart, but the game demands that players think smart too. The fact that even high handicappers are now able to shape shots allows courses to be set up to expect those shots, rather than having to make allowances for the poorer player.

Golfcross goals are laid out to exploit the oval ball's predictable flight properties. Narrow fairways, tight doglegs, and difficult goal approaches are the norm and demand an advanced level of strategic play.

Additionally, the course designer is assisted by being able to alter the shape of the yard and the facing position of the goal. These two variables alone provide a rich array of strategic options with which to challenge the player. Better still, because the goals are readily shifted and the yards quickly reshaped, designers are able to take risks and experiment with unconventional layouts, knowing that they can be easily changed if they're not working.

It's this flexibility that makes a golfcross course so simple and cheap to establish. There are no expensive greens to construct and maintain. Fairways are narrow and only need to be mown low enough to ensure that the ball can be seen. This means a golfcross course can be sited almost anywhere – even temporarily – with minimal effect on the environment.

But what about its effect on a golfer's game? With such a controllable ball, do players run the risk of becoming lazy? Evidently not. Most report that all the various lofted shots that Cross requires helps improve their short game, and not having to worry about slicing or hooking can have the effect of freeing up their swing.

Golfcross is certainly not remote control hitting. You still need a swing and all the other playing skills. There's also plenty of room for flair, experimentation and outright talent, just like in regular golf. In fact, far from being a threat to your golf game, golfcross has the potential to complement it.

The greatest threat to golf today is the rising cost of playing it. The huge capital investment required to construct a course and the turnover necessary to maintain it, translate into green fees which are beginning to price the sport out of the reach the young players it needs to attract.

It's possible that golfcross, with its low development and maintenance costs, may one day help to provide those less able to afford the price of a round with an opportunity to enjoy another way of playing the great game of golf.

Teenagers are taught how to position the golfcross ball.

12   Rolf Mills and George Studholme (right) playing golfcross at Wanaka in 1989.

THE MAKING OF THE GAME

The notion of developing a uniquely New Zealand game that would combine aspects of our two most popular sports, rugby and golf, had its genesis twelve years ago. Was it possible that a solid oval golf ball might have the same special flight properties of a rugby ball? Would it share the rugby ball's inherent gyroscopic stability which allows it to fly straight as well as being able to follow a variety of pre-set flight paths?

The idea was just too intriguing to leave alone and soon some crude oval balls made out of polyester resin emerged rather sheepishly from the garage workshop. They were like stones to hit but there was just enough aerodynamic potential in evidence to justify further tinkering.

Golfcross was first played with these same resin balls over Rolf and Lois Mill's Wanaka farm in the spring of '89. Using wooden rugby-style uprights with bird-netting stretched between them, Rolf Mills and George Studholme played a few hastily erected goals one sunny winter's afternoon as part of a photo shoot for a piece about unusual New Zealand pastimes. In fact the idea may well have died then and there at the photographic stage had it not been for George's enthusiasm for the concept. As the ex-green keeper for the local club he just loved the idea that all the expense involved with the construction and maintenance of greens could be done away with and with them gone, "you could play it very cheaply and just about anywhere – anywhere you can get a mower or a mob of sheep." Most of all, he loved the idea of the oval ball and felt it would be worth trying to get a proper one made. It took six years.

Golfcross Ball designs
1989 – 1997

5 6 7

1 2 3 4

8   9

1. Hollow, fiber-reinforced polyester resin ball, 1989. 50g.
2. Solid, polyester resin dimpled ball, 1989. 50g.
3. "Exploded" one-piece ball, St Andrews Golf Ball Co, 1991. 46g.
4. Lathed St Andrews one-piece balls, 1992. 33g & 27g.
5. One-piece blank, Penfold Golf, 1996. 46g.
6. One-piece blank, with drilled dimples & painted, 1996. 30g.
7. One-piece blank, Penfold Golf, 1996. 31g.
8. One-piece blanks, Penfold Golf, 1996. 45g & 57g.
9. Unpainted, dimpled ball, Penfold Golf, 1997. 50g.

Weight and shape are the two most important variables in the design of an oval golf ball. Weight determines the ball's ability to sustain spin, and shape impacts on how easily it can spin. The oval ball relies on a long spin time to maintain its various curving flight paths and it needs to be dense enough to achieve them but without feeling heavy off the club. Its overall shape — how thin or fat it is and whether the ends are rounded or pointed — determines how easily it slips through the air and therefore how quickly it spins.

Golf ball manufacturing is centered around just a few large companies who use high speed injection-moulding techniques which require a fortune in tooling costs for each design.

Unless you want to order a few million balls for a few million bucks you're not in the loop. Was it possible there might be a manufacturer producing low volume, compression-moulded runs who might be interested in dabbling with a number of shapes, sizes, and weights? Well, no. But the tiny St Andrews Golf Ball Company in Scotland, thoughtfully donated some oversize balls that had "exploded" out of the mould and had the appearance of fat Kinder Surprises. While hardly the shape envisaged,

they *were* one-piece composite balls. Could they be reshaped on a lathe? Joe Gibson, a local wood turner, kindly obliged and took great delight in chipping each different little oval shape round his back lawn as he lovingly completed each one. They were rather small these Gibson balls, and far too light, but we could still hit them 150 yards and therefore they could act as a guide to the way larger balls of the same shape would fly. What they needed now was some serious testing.

Enter the ideal collaborator – a man who truly loves golf and is passionate but never obsessive or narrow in his thinking about it. Martin O'Connor is one of those rare

golfers who can become totally absorbed in the game while somehow continuing to maintain enough distance to appreciate its subtle psychology and to see its funny side. In the final analysis it was probably his sense of humor and a fascination with the balls' high pitched hum that drew him into spending hours hitting them all over the local rugby ground. That, and the fact that the most oval of the balls completely confounded his every attempt to slice or hook it. There was definite potential here. All that was needed now was a full-sized ball to test.

Lots of international phone calls, lots of dead ends and then in October of '92 a couple of very special English gentlemen from Birmingham come on the scene – Peter Smewin and William Baird, production director and marketing manager of Penfold Golf, one of the world's oldest golf ball makers, and probably our last chance.

According to industry sources they have the technical know-how and the best one-piece composite formulations in the world, but will they be interested? Well they're certainly intrigued, but after much discussion over several months they finally decline saying that experimental moulding and small production runs are just not economically feasible.

More trips to Birmingham, more discussions and finally because they really believe it could work, they generously

decide to devote their own spare time to the project. It's not until 1996 that the first non-dimpled ball shapes are ready for trial. Nine months later the final shape, weight, compression and dimple pattern is decided on after an exhaustive testing program.

But now the whole project looks like falling over because it seems impossible to build a goal that can handle the kind of ferocious winds sometimes encountered on a course. Dominic Taylor, a young industrial designer who works in the film industry, thinks he can help. It's not an easy brief, even for someone whose last job was making a computer controlled robotic dog with forty-five articulated joint

movements. The goal has to turn, fold up, provide a ball capture system that's 99.9% efficient, repel cattle, be aesthetically pleasing, non-corrosive and above all, withstand 100mph winds. Success only comes after five prototpyes and numerous field trials.

Dominic's design philosophy centers on translating nature's forms into the mechanical environment. Knowing that smart trees stay upright by shedding branches in high winds, he designs a graceful structure with highly flexible branch-like stays that are tension hinged so as to collapse in on themselves when the going gets really tough. It works brilliantly, so course selection and design can finally proceed.

THE OVAL BALL

For many golfers constantly assailed with information about the importance of the golf ball's perfect roundness, it comes as a bit of a surprise to learn that the oval golf ball is more stable and significantly easier to control – the very opposite of what most would expect. Its less regular shape suggests it will behave unpredictably, when in fact its greater aerodynamic complexity is the key to its advanced performance capabilities.

The flight path of a round golf ball is primarily determined by the amount and direction of spin imparted by the club face. However, the oval ball almost completely resists any spin you may give it and instead, allows its flight pattern to be solely determined by the way you set it up. It's as if it does what you "ask" it to do *before* you strike it rather than doing what it does as the result of *how* you strike it.

Hitting it in the vertical position for example, will ensure a straight shot, no matter how much you try to slice or hook it, while angling it severely to the right or left will promote a controlled slice or hook. It's like playing with a smart ball that has a programmable memory. Provided you hit it cleanly it will comply with your set-up instructions. This adds a wide range of possible shots to your repertoire and allows you to concentrate on what shots to play, rather than worrying about how to play them.

The forces acting on a solid oval ball in flight are complex, but in general its special performance characteristics can be explained by the laws of gyroscopic inertia and the fact that it has *three* axes of spin as opposed to the round ball's *one*. The reason the ball struck in the vertical position travels

straight and resists any tendency to hook or slice is that as it tumbles backwards along its transverse axis, any longitudinal spin which could take it off course reverses its aerodynamic orientation every half revolution.

You can see this clearly if you hold the ends of the ball between your fingers and turn it clockwise as if drilling into your finger. At the same time tumble the ball forward and you will see that every half revolution it turns in the opposite direction along its long (drilling) axis. Clockwise for the first half and anti-clockwise for the second. Thus the aerodynamic effect of the spin along the long axis is cancelled out as it travels through the air.

Another reason the oval ball will fly straight or curve in a pre-set direction is because once it has been set spinning on a particular axis it will maintain its angle of orientation in space in the same way as a spinning gyroscope resists any force which tries to deflect it from its angle of rotation. If the ball's angle of rotation is straight then it will travel straight and if it's leaning over to one side then it will go to that side in the same way as an aircraft goes to one side or the other when it banks.

What ensures that the ball continues to be held at the desired angle throughout its flight is the speed at which it tumbles. The greater the speed of rotation, the greater the resistance to change from the original axis of spin. Thus, when you angle the ball over to one side for a curved shot, you must ensure that it leans neither forward nor backward. This creates the greatest amount of tumbling backspin and holds the ball on its original course.

The direction that an oval ball takes after it pitches is mainly governed by the laws of precessional motion. These state that when a rotating body is subjected to a torque which tends to alter its direction of axis, it turns at right angles to its main axis of spin in order to conserve angular momentum.

You can see a good example of this if you lay the oval golfcross ball horizontally on the top of a table and spin it vigorously with your fingers. As it spins it receives a sideways torque from the table top and suddenly turns at right angles to its original horizontal position, jumping up onto its end and spinning like a top. This is why the *snake* shot suddenly changes direction on landing.

Because it is perfectly round, there is only one way to position a golf ball but the oval ball can be positioned in many ways, each of which results in a different flight pattern. There are five basic positions that are used to achieve specific types of shot. There's *reflected* for straight, maximum-distance shots, *vertical* to stop the ball quickly, *angled* for curves, the *torpedo* for long low runs, and *horizontal* for punch shots and *yardwork*.

Spin the ball horizontally on a table and it will suddenly start spinning vertically due to lateral torque. **21**

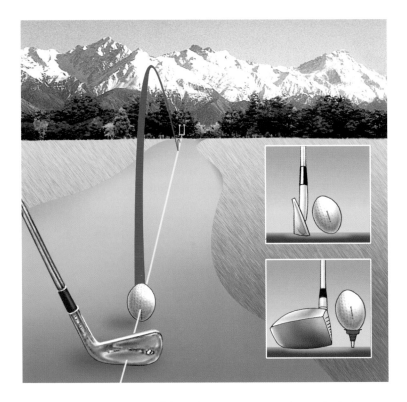

For maximum distance, position the ball vertically and then slope it straight back at the same angle as the loft of the club face. This is called reflecting because the angle of the ball closely reflects the angle of loft. The reflected ball carries farther because the club face makes full contact with it and promotes minimal backspin. This ensures less aerodynamic drag, a lower more efficient trajectory and no arresting backspin on pitching. The well struck shot flies straight, tumbling slowly backwards with a pulsating whooshing noise and no hum. You should be careful not to over reflect the ball by angling it back too far as this can promote topspin and cause it to dive.

The reflected ball has a low trajectory and travels farthest.

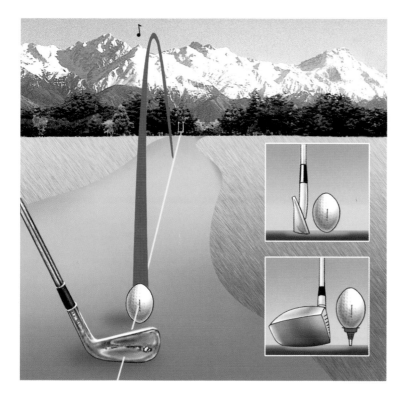

The vertical ball stops very quickly with any club.

To apply backspin so that the ball stops dead on landing, position it vertically. This allows the club face to strike below the center of the ball which means less club-ball contact and therefore less velocity but plenty of backspin. The ball flies straight, tumbling rapidly backwards with a high pitched hum – the higher the pitch, the greater the speed of spin and the shorter the flight of the ball. It has less carry than a reflected shot, a higher trajectory and a steeper angle of descent which, along with its backspin, means it stops very quickly – even with a 3-wood. For a better feel with the more lofted clubs, you can reflect the ball back a little and still retain sufficient backspin.

23

To hit a fade, position the ball vertically and then angle it over to the right to the extent of the fade required. Then hit straight through. It's interesting to experiment with fades and draws, angling the ball a little bit farther over to the side each time you hit it in order to see how much more it flies to that side. The more vertical the ball, the higher its trajectory will be, the farther it will carry and the less run-on it will achieve. On pitching, the ball will usually continue to maintain its direction of travel. When angling the ball to the side it's important that you don't also reflect it back as this will stop backwards spin and prevent it from maintaining its angle of rotation.

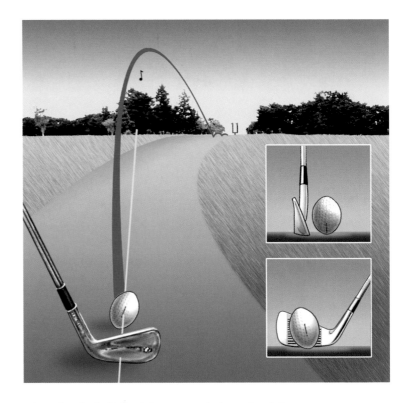

To make the ball fly right you angle it to the right.

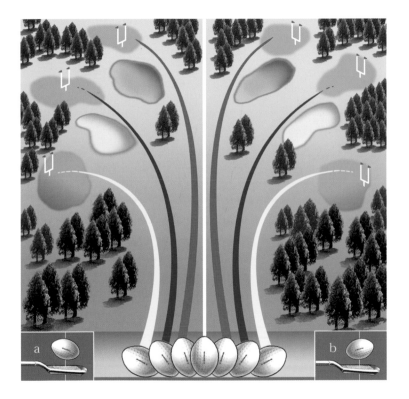

Hitting fades or draws and controlled slices and hooks is simply a matter of setting the spin axis of the ball. The farther over it is angled to one side the greater the movement will be to that side. You'll find that the more the ball is angled to the side the flatter its trajectory will be, resulting in a more oblique angle of descent with greater run-on. Also, the more horizontal the ball is the sweeter it will feel off the club. When using shorter irons (anything from the 8 down) controlled hooks (a) and slices (b) are best achieved by laying the ball horizontally and moving it into a ten-past-eight position for a slice and a ten-to-four position for a hook.

Fades, draws, and controlled slices and hooks are easily achieved.

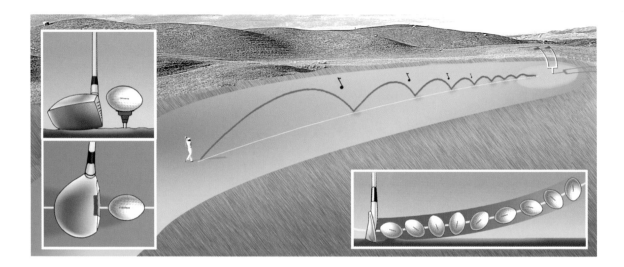

Because it's oval, you can strike the golfcross ball well off center and apply a great deal of top spin. The ball is laid horizontally with one sharp end pointed at the target like a torpedo and struck on its other end. It descends quickly and skips along on its ends in a series of giant humming leaps that carry it almost as far as the lofted ball. The high spin rate keeps the ball on track despite unevenness of terrain. This makes it a useful shot in high winds or when needing to keep the ball low under trees. [Best with woods and long irons.]

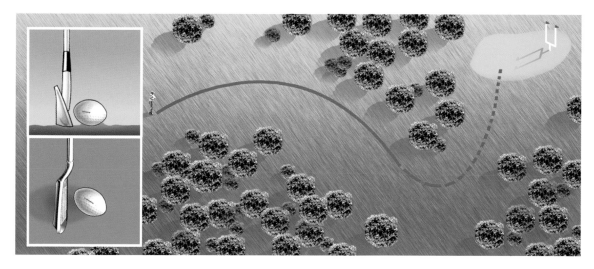

The snake shot travels one way in the air and the reverse on landing. Lay the ball in the torpedo position and then point its back end in the direction you want it to move. As with draws and fades, the more you move it to one side the farther to that side it will go. When you hit this shot the topspin forces the ball back to earth while it still holds a lot of kinetic energy. Whereupon it is subjected to a vigorous torque from the ground that drives it off in a series of curving bounces at 90 degrees from its original direction in the air.

Because the oval ball lying on its side makes contact along the length of the club face, it has the best feel and comes off hotter than the vertically positioned ball. However, the horizontal position is very sensitive to your swing plane and unless its long axis is exactly parallel with the club face it will tend to veer off. When hit straight it takes plenty of backspin which promotes good lift but tends left or right on descent. Raising its end just a few millimeters will promote a predictable draw or fade with a high trajectory. Because it maintains direction over short distances, the horizontal position is most effective around the *yard* and produces the best punch shot for goal.

28   The horizontal ball is swing-plane sensitive and tends to drift.

The oval golfcross ball in the reflected position is able to travel a shorter distance than the round ball because it presents a larger profile to the air.

The shorter the club the less the distance differential – usually around ten yards for a short iron and up to forty for a driver. The fact that it travels much straighter and not as far as a round golf ball is a boon to course designers as it enables fairways to be shorter and narrower. This means greater flexibility in the utilization of available land.

Because of its longitudinal shape, it's possible to hit the golfcross ball well below its center of mass. Even with a 3-wood you're able to promote a tumbling backspin that enables

it to stop very quickly on pitching. But this backspin does not result in the usual increase in lift and extension of hang time that we're used to with the round ball. This is largely due to the oval ball's irregular shape. As it tumbles through space it presents differing frontal profiles to the air which cause a constantly changing laminar flow around it. This reduces lift and promotes a lower, less wind-affected trajectory which still has the stopping power of a more lofted, backspun shot.

Flight performance is also affected by shape and dimple pattern. Future golfcross ball designs will still be determined by the need to maintain gyroscopic stability, while minimiz-

ing drag and ensuring the correct degree of lift.

The golfcross ball will tend to have fewer and deeper dimples to produce more efficient trajectories and have round rather than pointed ends to assist its tumbling action. While it will have noticeably less hang time, it should be short by a margin of at least ten percent over the distance achieved by the round ball.

Being more aerodynamically complex and therefore more stable in flight, most shots with the oval ball are fairly straight forward. Once you've learned the five basic positions: vertical reflected, angled, torpedo and horizontal, common sense will tell you how best to position the ball in various playing situ-

ations. When hitting out of the rough for example, the ball placed vertically clearly offers less resistance to the grass and will take backspin despite grass coming between ball and club. Similarly, knowing that the golfcross ball is able to resist sidespin tells you that it will fly straight from a sidehill lie and that there's no need to adjust your aim as you would with the round golf ball.

However, because the ball can't be moved in a hazard there are times when you'll need to know how to hit it if it's lying in an unusual position. Almost always when positioning the oval golf ball, you set it up so that it's not angled through more than one plane at a time. If it's reflected back

The oval ball in a hazard poses some interesting problems.

you don't also angle it to the side and vice versa. But in a bunker you will often confront a ball that's angled in two directions and you'll need to know where to strike it so that it goes towards the target. If you find the ball with its front end pointing to the right of the goal and its back end raised up, do you strike it straight along its horizontal face or do you approach it from behind?

There *will* be a right way, but whether you work this out or not, these situations make for interesting discussions on the golfcross course and add immeasurably to the intrigue of the oval ball.

Regardless of position, technique is the same as in golf.   **31**

THE GAME OF GOLFCROSS

Golfcross is golf with goals instead of holes and while its oval ball gives you the control of a pro, the game itself demands that you think like one too. This is no easy game for hackers. The ball might be smart but you still need to be able to hit it cleanly. You need touch, accuracy, correct club selection and all the other things that make golf such a wonderfully challenging sport.

Above all you need a good grasp of shot shaping because golfcross will present you with new strategic problems and a tactical match play component that's certain to add another dimension to your mental game.

With just a few exceptions and additions, golfcross uses the same rules as golf and has an identical scoring system. Each shot counts. A quick read of the rules and the glossary at the end of the book will give you a good overall feel for how it works. The main difference is that you're trying to hit a stable ellipsoid between eighteen sets of elevated *uprights* rather than an unstable sphere down eighteen holes. There are no greens and there's no putting. But there are yards marked out round each goal. Land your ball inside the yard and you're able to turn the goal to any one of three set positions. When you're outside the yard you have to *lay on* to get *turning rights* or attack the goal in its *facing position* by going for a *field goal*. If you're not in the *goal zone* you could take a *punt* and try to go in over the top.

Golfcross terminology may sound strange but essentially you're still playing golf. It's simply that the target is now more three dimensional and every shot is pretty much going where you want it to which is important because the fairways are narrow and there's only one way into the goal.

Because the flight of the ball is controlled by the way you position it, a durable, high-grip rubber *tee cup* has been developed to hold the ball at any number of different angles when teeing off. Both the tee cup and the ball should be clean and dry for maximum grip. In soft ground, the tee cup can be pushed in by first making a small hole with an ordinary golf tee or the back of a pen. When the ground is hard or a greater ball elevation is required, the tee cup can be stretched over most regular golf tees after either piercing the bottom of the tee cup with the sharp end of the tee or, for larger tees, cutting the nipple

off the bottom. The pointed end of the tee is then pushed through the hole that's formed in the bottom and the tee cup drawn up over it. With some tees it may be necessary to roll the top of the tee cup down so

that they fit firmly. If the tee cup will not hold the ball at the angle you require, try tilting it in the opposite direction to the angle and then lay the ball so that it is more in contact with the flared rim. Alternatively,

you can hold the ball at an extreme angle by pressing the tee cup over the point of the ball. The cup has been designed to suck firmly onto the ball whether used on its own or with a tee.

The flight path of the oval golf ball is dependent on how it's angled, so the rules of golfcross allow you to position it one foot from where it lies on the fairway or in the yard.

You can't use the tee cup but the oval ball is easily held at all angles by the grass and natural indentations in the ground. If extra elevation is required, a pitch repairer makes a useful tool for bringing up the turf and building a natural tee.

The goal is made of very flexible high tech materials which enable it to withstand extreme weather conditions. Its *chain* and *position locator* are of special importance to players.

The chain, which runs from a clip under the *crossbar* to the ground, holds the goal in the facing position. This is the position the goal mouth is facing when you tee off. The goal remains in this position until your ball is in the yard and is returned to this position when shooting from outside the yard.

Laying the ball in the yard (inside the *yard markers*) is important because it gives you turning rights – the right to turn the goal mouth to one of three locked positions. These are held by a cog mechanism

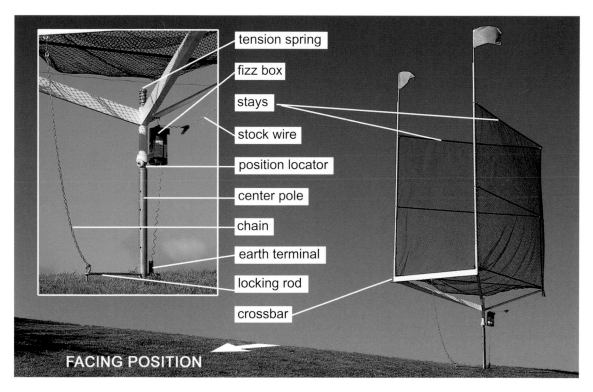

tension spring

fizz box

stays

stock wire

position locator

center pole

chain

earth terminal

locking rod

crossbar

FACING POSITION

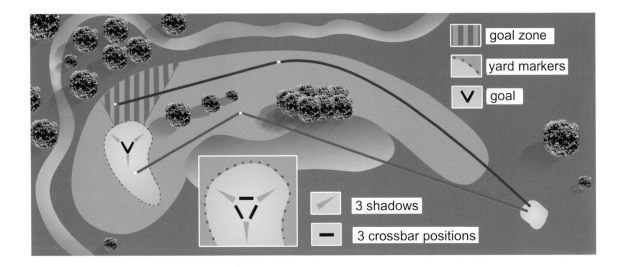

goal zone

yard markers

V goal

3 shadows

3 crossbar positions

called the position locator and you can't shoot for goal unless it's locked with its wheel in a valley. The chain must be re-clipped to the crossbar before players leave the yard. This

returns it to the facing position ready for the next players.

With its clearly visible flag-topped uprights stretching four meters above the ground, the goal appears temptingly large.

To most golfers used to a little hole and a pin, *goaling out* from anywhere closer than 100 yards looks like a distinct possibility. But hitting a ball through a tar-get suspended in mid-air is very different from landing it on a ground-based target and calls for new levels of judgment.

There's another problem that will also be new to golfers. Unlike the golf hole which can be attacked from all sides, there's just one way into the goal from the fairway and it's often only from a small area called the goal zone that a direct shot is possible. This area is marked with stripes on the course card along with the shape of the yard and the facing position of the goal so you know just what you're up against before you tee off. The triangular goal is represented by a <. Its open end is the goal mouth in the facing position.

But not only do you need to carefully consider your angle of approach to the goal, you must also know where to land in the yard as there are *shadows* or shade areas between the three fixed goal mouth positions. From here only an oblique shot at a reduced target is possible.

In the illustration opposite, Red decides to take on the pond and rewards himself with a short approach to the yard which slopes away to the river behind. Blue plays a draw and flirts with the stream in order to allow a longer second shot to the goal zone.

Both players must play their second approaches carefully. The closer Blue plays to the goal the smaller the goal zone becomes and the greater his chance of over or under shooting which will leave him with an oblique or no shot at all for his third. Red's second shot, while shorter, must nevertheless land in a smaller area than Blue's in order to get turning rights and he risks finding the shade at the back of the goal or going off the sloping yard and having to play back on.

Blue has the longer third shot and will target the pond side of the goal so as to avoid the slope and have plenty of yard to land in should he miss. If he does, he'll need another stroke to come back on without any chance of a goal. Red's third shot is oblique but there's plenty of goal zone out the back provided he keeps right.

Which is all quite a lot to think about before you stop to consider what club to use and

40   A punch shot to the back of the net can make tending the goal an exciting experience.

how you'll position your ball.

When really close to the goal (see rule 12) an out-to-in swing with an open faced wedge is the obvious choice. This shot requires a decisive follow

through and you should first check that your swing is clear of the crossbar and that you are ready for a possible rebound.

There are two options when goaling out from farther back.

Firstly, there's the flat, forceful punch into the back of the net with the ball in the horizontal position. The big advantage of this shot is that difficult height-over-distance calculations can

41

be dispensed with. All you have to worry about is direction. Failure, of course, may well see your ball bounding off the yard into big trouble.

You also need to watch for wind billowing the net in on one side. This tightens the net and makes it springy enough to bounce a strong punch right out again.

Second is the coddler (illus. p.92), a soft lofted shot with the ball positioned vertically or horizontally that falls gently into the basket. The advantage of this shot is that if it misses, the ball will stay in the yard.

yourself in a situation in which you are off the yard and only have a side view of the goal. The prudent course of action is to chip on and gain turning rights but for many golfers this approach will seem too timid. Instead they will take a punt and try to go in through the open top of the goal. It's the ultimate shot in golfcross and golf's equivalent of a flop shot off hardpan using a sixty-four degree wedge, and with only five feet of green to work with.

The degree of technical proficiency required is high and while many very good players will fail, they will at least play a lofted shot and it will fall safely at the base of the goal. Anyone less than good will be dicing with death. A poorly executed

But it does require you to be on good terms with your wedge. This is one of the hardest shots to play and without doubt the most important in golfcross. Time spent working on it at the practice goal will be well worthwhile.

Another shot worthy of practice is the punt. Because the goal has only one angle of approach you will often find

flop shot almost always has one result – a screaming shank that travels no more than a foot off the ground. But when the chips are down, taking a punt can pull you back from the brink of disaster. It's the most formidable shot to have in your arsenal, and definitely the most satisfying of all to pull off.

Equally satisfying is being able to turn against your opponent. *Turning against*, or *blocking off* as its better known, introduces a challenging tactical element to match play. It's based on one of golf's oldest rules – that the farthest away from the hole plays first.

In the illustration opposite, Red plays first because he's farther away and secures a handy goaling out position just out-

The player nearest us is in a position to block his opponent off.

side the yard. Seeing Red's position, Blue *lays away*, finds the yard and being at a greater distance from the goal, plays first. As he's in the yard he gets the right to turn the goal to a favorable position. If he goals out, and here's the rub, the goal will not be turned back to the facing position for Red when it's his turn as it would be in stroke play. It must stay in its last position. Red will now have to take a *country punt* or play an extra stroke to get onto the yard and receive turning rights.

Blocking off puts a premium on finding the yard and gaining maximum distance off the tee in order to play second. It also tempts players to take risks.

Not only has Blue flirted with the stream at the back of the yard in the hope of forcing a block but by laying away he has also given himself a longer shot at goal. If he misses and remains in the yard, he needs another shot at goal and so loses the one stroke advantage. Worse still, there's very little yard room at the goal end, so if he miscalculates direction or height he could run off the yard and be forced to play back to a goal that is now turned against him.

Clearly, golfcross match play calls for a calm nerve and the ability to think ahead.

When you step onto a golfcross course with an oval ball you need to leave a little of your golf knowledge behind. You will be playing with a genuinely smart ball which, despite appearances, is actually more aerodynamically stable than the round one you know so well. Amongst other things it will enable you to:

1. Hit the ball straight every time.
2. Perform controlled slices and hooks with ease.
3. Adjust the degree of fade or draw you require.
4. Impart backspin – even with a wood or out of the rough.
5. Apply top spin to achieve long low running shots and,
6. If you really want to show off, do double curves.

Just remember, on the golfcross course you may need all of these shots and more.

DESIGNING A COURSE

Golfcross courses don't need to be set up on farms. Almost any land is suitable. But the value of farms is that they come with farmers, and farmers have years of accumulated knowledge and understanding of land that is their livelihood and their love.

They know just where it's safe to site a riverside tee because they know just how high the water rises in a flood. They can tell you where the wind is worst and the soil is best, where it dries out in the summer and where it stays green. Above all they know about grass – how to grow it and how to look after it, and they have all the necessary equipment. In short, working in partnership with a farmer will make the process a whole lot easier and a good deal cheaper too.

When you design a golfcross course you need to follow the old wisdom of listening to the land. You'll need to walk all over it, viewing it from as many different angles as you can find because it takes time to seek out the challenging shots that the landscape offers up.

You also need to remember that almost any golfer who arrives to play with the oval ball will possess a range of shot making skills that have only ever been available to the experienced player. Your course should be designed to expect those skills. Fairways can be narrow and doglegs tight. Even tunnels of over-hanging trees can safely be brought into play. And as these golfers will have a lot less trouble executing the difficult shots you should ensure they spend more time judging them.

Here the workings of the goal and yard will arm you with a vast array of strategic possibilities to test the intellect, and create a challenging course.

48   No costly earthworks were required to create this farm course.

When clearing land for grazing, farmers often leave trees along stream banks to curb erosion and allow others to remain dotted about in the middle of paddocks to provide shade and shelter for stock.

Land like this provides a good deal of scope for natural design and enables fairways and yards to be sited where they'll fit rather than imposing a plan on the land.

The predictability of the oval ball's flight means narrow openings can be brought into play without the need to fell valuable trees and if the land is blessed with meandering waterways, challenging island yards can be created where a creek or stream turns back on itself.

A winding creek forms a natural island yard.

Most farms have ponds or small lakes to water stock and these can make an ideal hazard off the tee. When the goal mouth is in direct line with the tee, you have two choices. Either a long carry over the water with a driver that could reward you with a field goal on the approach, or less risky, laying up to the side which will mean a longer oblique shot at goal.

Farm buildings and stock yards like the stone ones on the right can guard the goal and make for an interesting obstacle. Features like these may be unconventional on a course but they are the essence of golfcross and remind us that the game and its terminology is tied to farming life.

50   The facing position can tempt players to flirt with danger.

The "yard" gets its name from stock yards like these.

52   Grazed land, with its clearly visible contours, quickly highlights its golfcross course potential.

Rolling sand hills like these drain well but retain enough moisture to support healthy grass which makes them perfect for golfcross. This sheep grazed country has deep rooted turf that gives it better access to nutrients during periods of stress. Compared to many golf courses where top irrigation and low mowing fosters a shallow root system, pasture is far more resilient.

The advent of the oval golf ball which allows for controlled backspin out of the rough, means that fairways only need to be mowed to a level where the ball can be seen. This goes a long way towards encouraging hardier grass that will keep its color and vigor longer during dry summer conditions.

A great benefit of the golfcross course is that it's not a static entity. Once set up, there's always ample scope to change it around if it's not working as well as it might.

Goals can be easily shifted and yards reshaped simply by repositioning yard markers. Perhaps the goal is too near a creek and needs to be moved ten yards to the left. Maybe a particular hump would work better inside the yard. Or would a smaller yard improve the goal? Possibly the yard needs to be expanded for a month or so to rest a worn area. It's a simple matter to change it.

Tees also need to be designed with flexibility in mind. If it's not possible to make a large enough tee area without carrying out extensive earthwork, you might consider setting up three or four smaller tees in the same area and swapping them around every week. You don't have to dismiss an elevated site with a wonderful view of the fairway just because it won't take more than a couple of weeks' traffic. Maybe there are several other areas it could work in rotation with.

Free-formed tees that blend in with their surroundings are preferable to ugly built up rectangles, and slightly more lateral slope than usual is permissible. This is because the oval ball can be hit from a cross-slope lie without favoring the low side as happens with the round ball.

This exquisite tee site, though small, can still be utilized by rotating it with other areas just below.

Ngawaro is a beautiful 9-goal farm course set among rolling hills forty minutes from Rotorua in the middle of New Zealand's North Island. The club was set up by a group of local farmers and is a great example of the way an existing golf course is able to accommodate golfcross and rotate playing days between it and golf according to demand.

A flock of 250 lambing ewes keep the fairways in excellent condition, with only a little additional mowing needed when spring growth exceeds their grazing capacity.

Like a lot of farm courses in New Zealand, each green is protected against stock damage by a low electric wire which runs around its perimeter. With

Goal shares with hole at Ngawaro, which offers golf and Cross.

good management, the sheep provide cheap maintenance in return for a profit from the sale of lambs and wool.

Goals and yards are set up to the side of greens and far enough away so there's little chance of balls landing on them. If they do, a free drop is taken from the edge of the green to ensure they're not damaged.

Another method of setting up golfcross on a golf course is to play the goals in the reverse direction from the holes. Teeing areas are provided near greens, and yards are situated near the golf tees. Playing a course backwards like this adds great interest and the oval ball's ability to handle tight corners allows dog-leg fairways to be easily played in reverse.

Ngawaro's 6th has a 100 yard carry off the tee over a lake.

Closely grazed sand hills formed long ago by old river systems, create a great range of challenging undulations on lowland farm courses like these. Even the most gentle rippling of swells and swales will provide the golfer with a wide variety of testing stances. When the land erupts in a series of steep rolling mounds, narrow winding fairways can be traced between their folds.

Some terrain that is unsuitable for mowing, can still be brought into play by managed grazing. Such areas could well prove contentious on the golf course, but they are far easier to handle with the oval golfcross ball which, as stated earlier, is not affected by cross-slope lies.

Even the slightest of undulations brings the fairway alive.

A sea of sheep-grazed hillocks sprinkled with trees provides wonderfully challenging goals. **59**

Coastal areas make ideal sites for temporary golfcross courses. A course can be quickly set up and easily dismantled with minimal effect on the environment. The goal only needs a ten inch diameter hole three feet deep to hold the center pole which supports the light aluminum goal frame.

Depending on the ground, hand-digging nine holes and concreting in plastic sleeves to receive the center pole only takes two people three days once the course has been worked out. Add another week for laying out yards and mowing and you can have a golfcross course up and running in two or three weeks. This makes it viable to set up a course in a dramatic coastal setting or even in a public park for a one-off weekend competition. When it's over the holes can be filled in, yard markers removed and the goals folded up and shifted to another site.

While the goals have been designed to handle harsh coastal conditions, fairways may need to be wider than the normal twenty yards as strong onshore winds can carry the ball into difficult terrain. But coastal land provides interesting and unusual hazards that make the temporary golfcross course a delight to play on.

A "fun" goal set up as part of a temporary seaside course.   **61**

A stretch of swamp grass can add to the visual impact of a goal as well as providing an interesting hazard. Grasses like these can also be used to define the general area of a yard.

Where golf has guidelines regarding the steepness of greens, Cross can have yards of almost any undulation, provided they're able to be mowed or effectively grazed.

Yards like these are particularly challenging but to be fair, you should always provide at least one area for a player to aim for which allows a relatively easy goaling opportunity.

Overshooting this yard on the wrong side can land you in all sorts of trouble.

When designing a golfcross course you'll be looking for tight fairway dog-legs that call for controlled hooks and slices. These can be readily achieved with the oval ball. The goal and yard can also be positioned to allow overhanging trees to flank the facing position and provide an obstacle within the goal zone. This will encourage an approach with the torpedo shot which sprints low and straight, and covers as much ground as the lofted vertical ball.

Sometimes a tree can even be included inside a large yard to provide a measure of strategy but you need to be aware that the goal could be damaged by falling branches and that players may face the risk of a

Overhanging trees encourage the torpedo shot.

deflection.

Natural yard areas can be formed by digging shallow ditches a few feet away from their perimeters. These not only keep the yard well-drained but they encourage rushes and long grass which help to make it more clearly visible from a distance.

Trees can't be used as obstacles close to golf greens because they cause root damage and their shade inhibits grass growth. With the yard these problems do not arise and they can effectively ring the general area of a yard provided there is an opening in the goal zone. Slow growing evergreens like these kahikatea opposite are ideal as they will not shed leaves onto the yard in autumn.

Yards can be ringed by rushes to help define them.

66   The goal's tall uprights help players get a fix on a yard hidden below the brow of a hill.

Designing a golfcross course in hilly country is made easier by the height of the goal's uprights. As these are tall, they can be tucked away in sheltered areas behind trees or below the brow of a hill with their flags still remaining visible from the tee. This helps avoid blind goals and means that a course doesn't have to confine itself to its valleys but can also wander over the hills in search of variety and new challenges.

On a farm course, deep grass bunkers which would normally be a maintenance nightmare, are kept well tended by grazing sheep.

The ultimate "Devil's Cauldron?"

TWO COURSES

Braemar Station and Station Bush couldn't be more different. One, bordered by the turquoise waters of a glacial lake and the Southern Alps, is wonderfully open to the sky. The other, nestled in the crook of a broad, lowland river, bathes in dappled light that filters through its many indigenous trees. What they share in common is an overpowering stillness that belies their agricultural purpose. Both are farms devoted to sheep and cattle and both are blessed with land that forms naturally into fairways and yards which beg to be played.

Bob and Barbara Smith, who have farmed Station Bush's 211 hectares for forty-five years, are avid golfers. Over that time they have often looked out at their lush green pastures studded with mature trees and imagined a golf course laid out on it. That dream could never be fulfilled because the river, which is the source of the land's fertility when its nutrient-rich waters flood over their fields at different times of the year, makes the maintenance of greens far too unpredictable. The advent of golfcross, which does away with greens and has specially

designed goals that can be tele-scoped well above the swirling floods, meant the course at Station Bush could become a reality.

Long popular with picnickers who come to enjoy its river views and shady groves, the property is just ten minutes from Martinborough, a small North Island town that is the hub of the region's wine growing industry.

Braemar Station, spread over 23,000 hectares on the eastern shores of Lake Pukaki has been farmed by Duncan and Caroline Mackenzie since 1969. Both keen golfers, their golf course began with just three holes set out round their homestead which they played with family and friends. It soon swelled to five and then nine before they adopted golfcross and laid out a new course with narrower fairways and challenging goal positions to suit the oval ball.

The ease of being able to shift goals or change the shape of yards allowed them to try different sites for the course before they came up with one that worked well and soon they plan to expand to a full eighteen goals.

It takes thirty minutes to reach the Braemar Station from either Lake Tekapo or Twizel in the heart of the South Island's alpine lake district.

Teeing off at Station Bush and goaling out at Braemar.

STATION BUSH

It's evident from the first glimpse of Station Bush, lying against the serpentine weave of the Ruamahunga River, that here is a jewel. The approach road leads you directly behind the 9th yard, and from this vantage point you can look down the fairway and to the rest of the layout beyond.

Rarely does the entrance-way of a sporting club offer such a visual feast. But at Station Bush the appetite is not merely whetted, it's honed to an almost desperate edge. Because of the immediacy of this initial view the need to begin play seems urgent and irresistible. However, for the first-time player coming to grips with the new ball it's crucial to spend time in the driving area before teeing off.

The 1st goal is not daunting. Indeed at 430 yards this par-5 offers a long and gentle introduction to golfcross. There's a chance to open the shoulders and test with some impunity the predictable flight properties of the oval ball. One side of the fairway is open for the less trusting golfer who wants to play safe. If, though, you are able to conquer the golfers' instinct to steer well clear of water and timber, you can take dead aim along the center cut, knowing that the correctly positioned ball will not bring the Kowhai-lined creek into play.

The 1st may appear to be uncomplicated but it's not merely an opening gambit in a nine-goal conversation – it's a teacher. And the very next goal will test you on your comprehension of yardage, club selection, and ball angling.

The 2nd is a classic risk-reward par-4. The creek that so dominated the first goal has now snaked its way back into contention by crossing the fairway at a nagging length from

the tee. The percentage shot is to lay up short of the creek which leaves an eight iron to the goal. But a well-struck fade off the tee could place you within easy striking distance of a field goal and an eagle.

After the par-3 3rd, Station Bush is transformed. The first three goals are played on gentle, if not flat, fairways. There's a groomed but slightly claustrophobic feel to this beginning. But over the next five goals you are transported into a landscape that is locally referred to as the Moguls. Apart from the breathtaking backdrop of the Tararua Ranges, the only respite from a tract of land that resembles the Southern Ocean in miniature, is a sparse collection of gnarled manuka. The

Torpedo under, coddler over or fade around at the 5th?

Moguls is totally exposed to the elements and this in turn, makes one feel slightly boundless and insignificant. Needless to say the rough on this part of the course is tigerish and unforgiving.

Admittedly there is an exquisite par-3 (the 120 yard 5th) at the far reaches of the course which offers a short return to a parkland layout. Over-shadowed by enormous poplars down the right side, you must hit a well thought out shot to find the yard which is almost hidden in a copse of kowhai.

But having been sufficiently humiliated by this tiddler, you once again resume your battle with the Moguls, in which the true value of the goals' facing

Cabbage trees are a feature of the 8th goal.

74   Kowhai Drive: A perfect finish to a round of golfcross.

positions and the location of the yards is exhibited to a nicety. The undulating, narrow fairways are deceptive. Past golf experience would tempt you to go with the natural flow. But on the 6th and 7th it's imperative to check the facing positions before teeing off because unless you choose the correct line you could be cut off from the goal.

The yards in the Moguls are also quite a test. They've been cruelly placed on a variety of uneven areas and offer no guarantee of success once you've found them.

This part of the course culminates in the 300 yard par-4 8th. It sweeps extravagantly to the left, and is guarded by manuka on one side of the fair-

Tall kahikatea guard the 2nd.

way, and almost velodromatic banking on the other. The yard is slightly elevated and protected by water hazards on three sides.

From here, a track runs along side the wooded creek and across a bridge to the 9th tee. There, laid before you is the goal you first saw from your car. This is among the most beautiful 375 yards of golfcross you'll ever encounter. It's only a kink or two from being a straight path to the yard beyond, but the trees on either side of what becomes an ever narrowing fairway, plus creeks guarding both flanks, makes this a sumptuous finale.

A glade of native evergreens borders the goal at the 1st.

BRAEMAR STATION

Braemar is something of an enigma. It has a geographically surreal quality to it and is like no other place on Earth. Yet there is also something familiar about it. It's reminiscent of Irish links and is one of those tracts of land that appear always to have had golf played on it. Best of all, though, it can be appreciated by golfers of any level. A player's course – and Braemar is certainly in this category – usually discourages the average to novice golfer because of its severity. But this is not the case here. The setting alone is inspirational. Add to this some unique golfcross

challenges, and you are left with a course that has universal appeal.

Most golf courses have a signature hole – one that is instantly remembered even years later. This hole becomes the club's advertisement. But at Braemar the goals are all memorable and one tends to recall the entire course as a unique test of skill rather than single out one specific feature.

This property has a remarkable set of natural goals and as early as the 2nd you are not only aware that this will be an extraordinary round but also that you are not playing golf.

The 2nd is a 256 yard blind, dog-leg par-4. It's set in a deep gully which is only five yards wide. In order to negotiate the final corner, the second shot demands a controlled slice with a short iron - a shot only possible with the unique flight properties of the Cross ball.

Walking down the par-5 3rd you are confronted with a sight seldom seen on a regular golf course. You have an unimpeded view of six goals. This phenomenon is partly because Braemar is a high-country tussock course and therefore devoid of trees. But the views of the layout are

chiefly possible because of the terrain. The 3rd, 7th and 8th goals all border a huge triangular-shaped gully (fondly referred to as the Braemar Triangle by locals because of the number of balls that disappear into its depths). From any one of these goals you can look across to the other two and see them almost as cross sections of fairways.

The 3rd goal, however, is spectacular on its own account. It's almost two goals in one because from the tee it resembles a downhill ski slope favoring the fade, and covers 496

80

yards of narrow terracing. But given the shorter distance of the oval ball, two well-struck shots should still see you playing your third from the edge of the last terrace to a yard that is 130 yards below. Suddenly this par-5 is transformed into a pseudo par-3 drop goal. Long grass to the right and behind the yard act as a deterrent to over-clubbing, but nonetheless, it's hard to imagine a more exhilarating approach to a long goal.

And then there is the 5th. This par-5 will test both your concentration and your faith that the oval ball will fly straight. The views from the tee are at their most dazzling and can act as a major distraction to the hardest goal on the

(p.80) Looking across to the 7th.   (Above) The 2nd

Mount Cook: The 9th goal

course which runs along the lakeside in a series of dune-like hummocky hills. Landing zones for the tee-shot and second shots are small, so accuracy on this goal is at a premium.

To offset the rigors of these two fiendish, long goals, the layout at Braemar is punctuated by the 4th and 6th goals, but they offer only marginal relief. At 143 yards and 132 yards respectively, they demand good judgment in terms of distance, especially as they are exposed to the prevailing nor'wester. But it's the yards themselves that pose the greatest threat. The 4th is elevated and nestled in a basin which makes it blind from the tee. Taking dead aim for goal and overshooting would be tragic.

But equally, laying up in the goal zone will leave you on uneven ground. The 6th yard is situated on side sloping, and makes for an awkward stance when trying to goal out.

The 7th and 8th goals are classic examples of the maxim that par-4s don't need to be long to be challenging. They finger their way around the edge of the aforementioned gully and while there is ample room to play safe, the strategic facing positions of the goal-mouths force players to take risks if they want to make birdies.

And so to the last. The 9th tee sits astride a ridge from which every goal is visible, including, of course, its own. It looks inviting. It lies in a natural

The 5th runs along the shores of Lake Pukaki towards Mount Cook.

basin between two knolls, and the magnificent Mount Cook is directly behind. The temptation is to ignore the severe sloping to the center and left of the fairway and just take the direct route to the yard. But at 372 yards, the 9th will eat anything other than a carefully planned tee-shot to the right. And even in position A, the second shot is imposing. The yard is indeed lying comfortably between two knolls but what you can't see from the tee is that the ground behind the goal falls away to oblivion. This is heart-in-the-mouth stuff, and the perfect final challenge to an extraordinary course.

For New Zealand golfcross information and course details visit: www.golfcross.com

Teeing off from the 14th on the new eighteen goal test course

ETIQUETTE

All the usual rules of golfing etiquette apply in golfcross, with the following additions and exceptions.

Chaining up: Re-attaching the chain to the crossbar after all players have goaled out is one of the most important rules of etiquette in golfcross. The chain can only be attached when the goal is in the facing position, thus ensuring it is ready for the next players. Failure to leave the goal in the facing position is similar to forgetting to return the pin to the hole in golf. Players seldom forget to pick up the chain and clip it back onto the crossbar but if they do, it can put those that follow at a disadvantage. This is because the next players must either walk up and turn it to the correct position before teeing off or accept the position it has been left in as the facing position (which may be more or *less* advantageous to them). A note reminding players to *chain up* before leaving the yard is often included on signs which mark the direction of the next tee.

Care of the land: While some golfcross courses will be purpose-built on land dedicated specifically to the game, most form part of a working farm and it is worth noting that the farmer who owns it is dependent on it for his livelihood.

Players should be respectful of the farmer's land, equipment and livestock. Fences should be crossed at stiles provided and if no stile or gate is within reasonable distance, wire fences may be climbed but only at a heavy strainer post. Gates should be left open or closed as they are found and players are encouraged to inform the property owner of any damaged gates, fences, equipment or any livestock in distress. But remember that the golfcross course is still a proper course and divots should be replaced etc.

Goals: The goal is an expensive piece of equipment and should be treated with the same regard that golfers treat a green.

Goal damage: Any damage or malfunction of a goal (eg. torn netting), should be reported as soon as possible.

Goaled balls: In order to speed up yardwork, balls are not usually removed from the goal until the last player has goaled out.

Coming on: In stroke play,

whenever a player plays from outside the yard, the goal must be in the facing position. While a player on the yard may be farther from the goal than the player off the yard and should therefore play first, it is usual for players off the yard to be invited on first so as to avoid unnecessary goal turning.

Tending the goal: Players tend the goal for each other with the first player to goal out usually tending for all the other players in order to avoid slow play.

Dress: Dress for comfort. Golfcross has no dress code.

RULES

All the rules of golf apply in golfcross, with the following additions and exceptions.

1. Teeing: Unless local rules permit, tee cups may only be used on the teeing ground.

2. Placing: On all fairways a player may pick up and position the ball within one foot (305mm) from where it lies and not nearer the goal or into the yard.

2a. In the yard the ball may be positioned but only where it lies.

2b. A player may build a tee on the fairway and in the yard.

2c. A ball may not be positioned in a hazard.

3. Hitting a moving ball: If a ball in play moves after it is addressed, it may be repositioned without penalty.

4. Immovable obstructions: A free drop of two club lengths not nearer the goal is permitted when the ball comes to rest in such a way as to impede the stance or swing of a normal shot because of an immovable obstruction. These obstructions include fences, gates, operative farm implements, water troughs and salt blocks.

5. Farmer's leavings: These are defined as any equipment or other immovable objects which are in a temporary position and obstructing a player's swing or stance. A free drop of two club lengths not nearer the goal is permitted to gain relief from fencing equipment, hay bales, cut firewood, storm damage, tractors, ploughs etc.

6.The yard: The yard is defined by yard markers which encircle the perimeter of the goal at regular intervals.

6a. A ball is considered to be in the yard if any part of it lies over a string line stretched between the outside edges of two adjacent yard markers.

7. Turning rights: When a player's ball lies within the confines of the yard, that player has the right to turn the goal to one of three locked positions before taking a shot at goal.

7a. The player whose ball lies farthest from the goal has first shot at goal regardless of whether his ball is in the yard or not.

7b. In stroke play, whenever a player's ball is outside the yard, he or she must play to the goal set in the facing position. This

Use a club (*yardstick*) or string to check if the ball is in the yard. **89**

rule applies even when the goal has already been turned to accommodate a player whose ball lies within the yard and has played first because they were farther away from the goal.

7c. In match play, once the goal has been turned, a player outside the yard must play to whatever position the goal is in, regardless of whether it is in the facing position or not.

7d. When playing to a goal that has not been returned to the facing position (not chained up) by previous play-ers, players must return it to the facing position before attempting to shoot for goal. This, however, may be subject to a local rule. See also rule 9.

8. Playing out of turn: If a player plays out of turn, they may be asked by another player to replay their shot without incurring a penalty. The player must be asked to replay the shot before another player has played.

9. Foul shot: In stroke play if a player shoots to the incorrect facing position from outside the yard, he or she must replay the shot without penalty. However, if this illegal shot is not discovered until the goal has been completed, a two shot penalty is incurred.

10. The goal: will have two uprights supporting a net no more than 2.4m tall rising from a crossbar no less than 1.24m from the ground. The uprights will be no more than 1.8m apart and topped with clearly visible flags. The goal will be held by a center pole fitted with a position locating device which allows the goal to be turned to one of three equidistant locked positions. (See illus. p.90).

11. Scoring: A goal is scored when the ball is struck by a player and comes to rest within the confines of the goal, (unless there is an appeal, see "Playing Out Of Turn" above).

10b. If a ball enters the goal and comes out again, it is still in play.

12. Free drops: when a ball lies within two club lengths of the center pole of the goal, relief may be taken by a free drop two club lengths in any direction from the center pole.

12b. If a ball becomes lodged on the outside of the goal between a stay and the netting, (a *cling-on*), a player must remove the ball and make a drop two club lengths in any direction from the center pole with no penalty.

RULES PENDING

The ball: No specification limits have yet been set by the NZGCA but it seems likely that balls will not have diameters less than 38 x 55mm and weigh no more than 52g.

92   "Coddling" the ball into the goal

GLOSSARY

Angled: The spin axis of the oval ball is set when it is angled to the right or left in order to determine its flight path.

As-good-as-goaled: Expression denoting an easy shot positioned right in front of the goal mouth.

Basket: See goal (ii).

Blocking off: Tactic used in match play to gain turning rights before an opponent enters the yard.

Center pole: The pole which holds the goal above the ground.

Chain: A length of light metal chain used to locate the facing position of the goal.

Chain up: To pick the chain up and re-attach it to the eyelet under the crossbar after all players have goaled out in order to ensure that the goal is returned to the facing position.

Championship goals: Narrow goals which make scoring more difficult.

Championship yards: Yards having an additional inner ring of different colored markers which define an alternative smaller yard area used in championship play.

Cling-on: A situation in which the ball is lodged between a stay and the netting on the outside of the goal.

Coddler: A soft shot with maximum loft designed to stay in the yard if it misses the goal.

Country punt: A shot for goal taken from behind the goal. The hardest shot in golfcross.

Cross: Short for golfcross.

Crossbar: The horizontal bar which connects the base of the two uprights.

Double yards: Two differently configured yards marked out around the same goal position to provide alternative yards on a nine goal course where an eighteen goal layout is required.

Drop the chain: Releasing the chain from the crossbar in order to turn the goal. Requesting a player to "drop the chain" is another way of asking them to tend the goal.

Egg: Slang term for the oval golfcross ball.

Facing position: The fixed position that the goal mouth is facing when a player tees off. (This position is secured by the chain).

Field goal: Ball played into the goal from outside the yard.

Field play: "Good field play" describes a player's ability to be able to consistently score field goals.

Fizz box: A battery operated charger attached to the center pole which provides an insulated wire around the goal with sufficient current to deter cattle from rubbing against it. When fitted, players should assume it's live and avoid touching the wires.

Fully engaged: See "locked."

Goal: (i) area between tee and yard. (ii) The posts and netting into which the ball must be played.

Goal frame: Triangular frame which turns on the center pole and supports the uprights, stays and netting.

Goaling out: Completing a goal.

Goal-in-one: A ball played into the goal from the tee. .

Goal zone: The vector outside the yard from where the clearest shot to the goal may be taken.

Horizontal: Ball position in which the ball lies horizontally with its long, flatter side facing out towards the target.

Humdinger: Ball struck in the torpedo position, usually with a driver, creating the maximum possible amount of topspin and the highest pitch of hum. Each time the ball comes into contact with the ground and "dings" along, its spin rate is reduced together with the pitch of the hum. (It is possible to achieve up to six clearly defined, descending notes as the ball bounces towards its destination).

Hummer: Ball rotating along its transverse axis (tumbling) which makes a humming sound that is higher in pitch the faster it rotates.

Laying away: In match play, hitting the ball into the yard but keeping it at a greater distance from the goal than one's opponent's ball when their ball is outside the yard, in order to gain turning rights and block them off.

Laying on: Hitting onto the yard in order to receive turning rights.

Locked: A goal is "locked" when the wheel on the center pole is located in a valley on the position locator fixed to the goal frame.

Locking rod: Ground level rod which stops the center pole from turning.

Position locator: Sprung device uniting a wheel on the center pole with a cog ring on the goal frame. This holds the goal in one of three equidistant positions.

Punt: Lofted shot in which the ball enters the goal through the open triangular top of the goal rather than between the uprights.

Reflected: Ball placed vertically on its sharp end and tilted back so that it "reflects" the club's loft.

Restricted turning rights: A stroke play option in which only two goal positions are allowed – the facing position and one other.

Shade, in the: See Shadows.

Shadows: The three sectors of the yard from where only an oblique shot at goal is possible.

Skip-round: Series of sideways bounces taken by the ball on pitching when it has been hit while positioned at an angle to the right or left of the target.

Snake: Ball hit in the torpedo position while angled to the left or right. The ball curves one way in the air before pitching and then the other way when bouncing.

Stays: Flexible rods which provide a triangular framework for the goal netting.

Tee cup: Hollow rubber cone which enables the oval

ball to be held at an angle. It may be used on its own or fitted onto a regular golf tee.

Tending the goal: Turning the goal for another player and ensuring that it is locked.

Torpedo: Ball in horizontal position with its sharp end

facing the target.

Turn against: In match play, when the goal is turned against an opponent who is outside the yard. See Blocking off.

Turning rights: A player's entitlement to turn the goal to one of three locked positions when his ball lies within the yard.

Unchained: Goal with the chain unattached and therefore probably not in the facing position.

Uprights: The two vertical poles which define the front edges of the goal.

Vertical: Ball position in which the ball stands vertically on its sharp end.

Yard: An area around the goal designated by markers.

Yard markers: Painted discs or pegs which define the perimeter of the yard.

Yardstick: The longest club in the bag, usually the driver, used to lay between the yard markers as a quick way of determining if a player's ball is within the yard.

Yardwork: Play within the yard including goal turning.

ACKNOWLEDGEMENTS

Golfcross is blessed with many people to thank – folks who have generously given their time, their knowledge and their encouragement to this project over the last twelve years. In particular, Dominic Taylor whose understanding of the mechanics of movement gave golfcross its wonderful goal and Martin O'Connor whose depth of golfing knowledge and love of its environment – he wrote the two course descriptions for this book – ensured that it stayed on track and remained true to the great game of golf. Heather Busch whose unstinting assistance and design flair saw this book through to completion. And Melissa, my partner in love and crime who's had to live with this game for as long as we've been together. Her belief in it and her constant support has given it wings. How far it will fly nobody knows but without all these good people to help keep it warm, it could never have progressed beyond the little white egg that was laid a long time ago in an old workshop by the sea in Wellington, New Zealand.

Mike Adams, William Baird, Chris & Jenny Bargh, Robbie Bargh, Greg Bartlett, Tony Bayliss, David Beaglehole, Jeremy Bicknell, Ian Biggs, Peter Camp, Luke Cartnell-Gollan, Ricky Cheng, Jan & Eddie Clarke, Ted Colton, Barrie Cook, Jim Copeland, Dominic da Souza, Peter Dengate-Thrush, Lana Doyle, Joe Gibson, Jack Gower, Carla Grey, Anne Firmin, Piers Faircloth-Harding, Kathy Hashimoto, Gus Hayden, Louise, Michelle & Russell Hight, Warren Hoy, Peter Irving, Ross & Helen Ivy, Lloyd Jones, Dick & Jillian Jardine, Dick Joyce, Stephen King, Russell Kirk, Arthur & Lyn Klap, Alan Knowles, Ray Labone, Hugh & Biddy McCarroll, Duncan, Caroline, Hamish & Annabel Mackenzie, Alister McLeod, Keith McLeod, Jim Mason, Rolf & Lois Mills, Andy Monson, Geoff Nutting, Colin Parkin, Sam Peters, John Pettigrew, Trevor Plaisted, Shaun Scott, David Shillson, Harry & Sarah Silver, Tina Symmans, Jeremy Simpson, Wayne Simpson, Peter Smewin, Bob, Barbara, Tim, Amanda & Dan Smith, Tom Southern, George Studholme, Stuart Thompson, Garrick Tremain, Annelies Vanderpoel, Paul Van Ooman, Neil Weighell, Harry Weir, Greg West-Walker, Kate White, Brian Wilkins, Alan & Alison Wilkinson, Joy Willis, & Phil Wood.

For more information about golfcross and to order balls, visit the website: **www.golfcross.com**